"Whatever the mind can conceive and believe, it can achieve."
-Napoleon Hill

Thank You

This journal is dedicated to my amazing wife. ***Thank you*** for being the strongest and most positive person I know. Despite all of the obstacles that are thrown at you, you always see the positive side of everything. ***Thank you*** for always being by my side and for lifting me up on the days where I am not so positive myself. ***Thank you*** for showing me a whole new world. This book was inspired by you and your amazing heart. ***Thank you*** for always seeing the beauty in life, and for always pushing me to be my best self. I love you.

I also want to thank my family and friends for all of their guidance and support, always.

I am especially grateful for the tremendous amount of support and guidance I've received from David Kasneci. Thank you for showing me this is possible and for believing in my ability to do this.

This journal is dedicated to **you**.

Thank you for choosing positivity, for deciding that today is the day you are going to change your mind and your life. My hope is that positivity and gratitude fill your mind and your heart and that you discover a new world with abundant opportunity and blessings, just as I have.

Reprogramming

33 DAYS. That is how long it takes to make a new routine a habit!

"We become what we want to be by consistently being what we want to become each day."
- Richard G. Scott

I've created this journal to help people understand that there is so much more to life once you see it through a new lens. I was once that person who was always negative. I didn't think I was, nor did I mean to be. But in some ways, it just came naturally (or so I thought). I would turn a positive thought into a negative one right away because I was "just being realistic!" I would say things like "Yeah, but you need to be practical, it won't work or it won't happen like that." How many of you have caught yourselves doing the exact same thing? Well, that is why "My Positive Mind" exists, to change your perception of reality and to show you that anything is truly possible.

In this journal you will learn about the power of the mind, energy and positive thinking. You will learn how to turn your negative thoughts and feelings into positive ones. And most importantly, you will learn about the power of gratitude! We will work together to make it a habit of thinking positively, to reprogram our minds to flush out all of the negative thoughts or habits, and replace them with positive ones. After all, the same amount of energy is required to demand abundance and prosperity than to accept unhappiness and scarcity. The choice is yours.

Everything is Energy

"I accumulated small but consistent habits that ultimately led to results that were unimaginable when I started."
- James Clear

I want you to read that quote again. I want to instill this quote in your mind. We are going to start, little by little, each and every day. By the end of this journal and this journey, you will look back and say, "This was unimaginable when I started!" We will open the mind to gratitude, energy and positive thinking. When we think positively, and feel gratitude, the universe works in our favor – it matches our energy. Life and all its possibilities become endless when our mind, body and soul are in the right state.

To achieve this balance between our mind, body and soul – we must learn to take control of our minds (subconscious and conscious) in order to take control of our lives.

To begin, it is important to understand Quantum physics, which is the study of matter and energy at the most fundamental level. Essentially, Quantum physics tells us that that everything in this Universe is made up of energy. You and I are made of energy. Every organ, tissue and gland in our body is made up of cells which consist of atoms. Atoms are made up of energy (electrons, protons and neutrons).

Did you know? You can actually see your body as energy with Kirlian photography, a form of photography that photographs the density and color of energy. If you enter a completely dark room, you'd see your whole being as a glistening form.

Everything is Energy

The universe itself is made up of matter, which consists of atoms and boils down to energy. All matter is made up of energy.

Now that we understand everything is made up of energy – it is important to understand how energy works:
Energy cannot be created nor destroyed, meaning the total amount of energy and matter in the Universe remains constant, it will never change! However, energy is always moving and can change form, so all of the energy in the Universe is constantly changing from one form to another. This is important to understand because EVERYTHING is energy, including thoughts. Thoughts are a form of energy and when that energy changes form, it manifests into the physical world.

Andrew Carnegie said, "Any idea that is held in the mind, that's emphasized, that's either feared or revered will begin at once to clothe itself in the most convenient and appropriate form available." Essentially, Carnegie was saying "Any idea you are constantly thinking about, whether it is good or bad, will eventually manifest in physical form." This is energy flowing to and through you, from one form to another.

From thoughts to things.

As energy flows into your consciousness, you start to visualize your thoughts, you internalize them (feel them) and eventually manifest them in physical form. This has nothing to do with reason or logic and everything to do with law.

Everything is Energy

The truth is – thoughts become things. Think about it, everything you currently have was once only a thought before it was a thing! Your clothes, your shoes, your TV, your phone, everything. It started out in the mind and then manifested into physical form.

So, if thoughts become things and what you think about manifests into physical form, why are you stuck?

Unfortunately, most people go through life without ever learning that they hold the power to change everything. We are taught so many things in life, through formal education or otherwise, but we're rarely taught about the importance of our own thoughts and how to choose them.

That is why you're here.

Most of you reading this have probably heard about "The Law of Attraction" which focuses on your thoughts and feelings to attract what you want into your life. However, most people believe The Law of Attraction is about saying what you want to happen and believing it until it happens. While part of that is true - The Law of Attraction comes down to energy and there is a law that comes before this one - that is "The Law of Vibration".

Understanding The Law of Vibration will help you better understand The Law of Attraction and thus allow you to manifest anything into existence with grace and ease. This is because you can only attract the things that are in harmonious vibration with you.

The Law of Vibration

The Law of Vibration states that nothing rests, everything moves. This movement is what we refer to as vibration. The speed at which something vibrates is known as its frequency. The difference between one object and another is the rate of its vibration, also known as its frequency.

According to the laws of energy and the law of vibration, everything is moving - including objects we perceive as 'static', like chairs and tables for example. These objects vibrate at an extremely slow speed/low frequency.

As noted, your thoughts - like everything else in the universe - are energy and they vibrate at different frequencies depending on the thought. Your thoughts lead to your feelings, and the combination of the two control the vibration of your body. Similarly, all of the things we want are also made of energy, constantly vibrating at a specific frequency.

The Law of Attraction focuses on 'like attracts like'. Attraction itself is force acting mutually between particles of matter (energy) to draw them together and to resist their separation.

Therefore, your feelings - which dictate your body's vibration - attract people and things to you that are a vibrational match (because like attracts like).

The Law of Vibration

So the things you want can either move towards you or away from you. If you are constantly worrying about what you want or doubting the fruition of what you want – the Law of Vibration says these things will move away from you, because your thoughts are not in harmonious vibration with what you want. However, if you have a vivid positive image in your mind of what you want and you feel confident that it is already yours, it will be!

So back to the question earlier – if thoughts become things and what you think about manifests into physical form, why do so many feel unhappy and stuck?

It's because we need to learn how to put ourselves in the right vibration. The Law of Attraction can only bring you what you match with. If you are constantly afraid, anxious or stressed you cannot attract joy, love and abundance. You're not an energetic match.

The great news is you have a choice! You can choose your thoughts. You may be thinking you choose your thoughts daily, but the truth is, most people don't choose their thoughts. They let their senses and outer circumstances dictate their thoughts and feelings. As a result, they live in a cycle of the same circumstances because they are vibrating at the same frequency.

When you learn how to choose your thoughts, you can choose your vibration and therefore attract anything - because everything is vibrating and once you match the frequency of what you want - the law of attraction will bring it to you.

The Power of Gratitude

So, how do we choose our thoughts? We start with gratitude. When you **feel** grateful and maintain that feeling, you raise your vibration, and you attract more to be grateful for.

Queue 'My Positive Mind' – a journal created to change your thoughts, feelings and habits, to teach you to choose good thoughts on a daily basis, to stay emotionally involved with these good thoughts and raise your vibration to attract everything you've ever wanted.

Abundance, wealth, love, health – everything you ask for because everything is here. Nothing is created nor destroyed, everything you want is already yours if only you vibrate in harmony. After all, you don't attract what you want; **you attract what you are.**

Remember, our bodies are vibrating at a frequency based on our thoughts and feelings. We may say we want something or we will receive something, but we will only truly attract what we are vibrating at the same frequency with. It's all about harmonious vibration - so choosing your thoughts and feelings carefully is crucial if you want to change your life.

Here lies the importance of a daily gratitude practice! A practice that is so often overlooked but has the ability to change everything. I know this, because practicing gratitude is what changed my life. It started with a change in habit, which led to a change in perspective, and eventually to major life changes.

The Power of Gratitude

"It's a funny thing about life, once you begin to take note of the things you are grateful for, you begin to lose sight of the things that you lack."
- Germany Kent

This quote, while deceptively simple, encapsulates profound truth. Unfortunately, its simplicity often leads people to overlook its depth. But truly, life can be so much simpler than we make it.

Let's start with perception. Perception is everything, it's like the age old metaphor of viewing a glass as half-empty or half-full. Technically, both views are correct. The key here is that you have a choice in how you view the glass, and how you view the glass is directly correlated to the amount of gratitude you have/express.

As previously mentioned, the law of attraction brings you more of what you are currently thinking/feeling. You may believe that life is difficult, stressful and overwhelming or you may believe that life is exciting, wonderful and full of incredible surprises. Whichever you believe, you will receive. So, if you believe that life is difficult, stressful and overwhelming, it will be hard to view the glass as half-full at first. In other words, it will be hard to express gratitude, when you can only see the world around you as half-empty. The law of attraction is precisely the reason this is so hard, because it's continuously bringing you more thoughts and experiences that align with your negative views. When you are complaining, you are ungrateful. This is not meant to be harsh, only to show you why you are feeling the way you feel. You're so focused on what you lack that you lose sight of all that you have.

The Power of Gratitude

Since you're focused on what you lack, the law of attraction brings you more lack. And because the law of attraction is law, it does not know that it is bringing you more of what you don't want, it only knows that it is bringing you that which you align with energetically. So how can you change this?

Gratitude.

Gratitude is truly the key to happiness. As Germany Kent said so simply, "once you take note of the things you are grateful for, you begin to loose sight of the things that you lack." Why? Because when you focus on what you are grateful for, the law of attraction will no longer bring you lack, instead, it will bring you more to be grateful for! I've experienced this first hand, because when I am truly grateful, I have nothing to complain about. Gratitude is a **feeling.** And when you truly feel the feeling of gratitude, you cannot help but be joyful, appreciative and blessed.

Gratitude isn't just some "spiritual mumbo jumbo." It is scientifically proven to elevate essential neurochemicals within the brain and body. As thoughts transition from negative to positive, there is a notable surge in the release of beneficial chemicals like dopamine, serotonin, and oxytocin. These substances collectively contribute to fostering feelings of closeness, connection, and overall happiness associated with gratitude. And just like anything, the brain changes with experience. So, the more one incorporates gratitude into their routine, the more the brain adapts to tune in to the positive in the surrounding world.

The Power of Gratitude

Now you know, in order to attract and manifest, you must be grateful for what you already have/where you already are. When you feel gratitude, you will continue to attract it.

The purpose of this journal is to make positive thinking and gratitude a habit, so that you are always in harmonious vibration with your desires. Like any habit, it will become automatic over time!

Over the next few pages, I've created example journal entries as a guide for what's to come. Each week, we will begin with a goal for that week and steps to take to reach that goal. I recommend starting with a simple goal, such as being consistent with this journal - after all, results don't work unless you do!

We will also list some affirmations for the week. Affirmations are powerful statements that will change your life. They're sometimes referred to as auto-suggestion or self-talk. Napoleon Hill referred to affirmations as the direct route of communication between the conscious and subconscious mind. Essentially, you are giving orders to your subconscious mind. Think carefully about the affirmations you want to use – who and what do you want to be? Write down a statement indicating that you are already in possession of this. Repeat this a few times and then read these statements out loud one by one and take a deep breath after each statement. If you can, close your eyes and feel happiness and gratitude for being this. Come back to your weekly affirmations daily, repeat them and feel them as much as you can. Remember, feeling is vibration!

Creating Habit

Every day, we'll start by stating five things we are currently grateful for and why. It's important to note that our current reality is the result of our previous thoughts. This is why our current thoughts must reflect our future desires – what we want our reality to be. Gratitude is the key. The goal is to choose 5 different things every single day, so that over the course of 5 weeks, you do not repeat anything.

Following the five statements of gratitude, we will choose a negative thought, problem or situation that we want to change. We will let go of the negative thoughts here. Breathe them out after you write them and let them go for good. I like to look at this as a statement of surrender. For example, "I am letting go of my worries" and giving these worries to God/Source/The Universe.

Finally, we will reprogram our current thoughts. Here is where we will ignore the 3D senses and tap into the power of our imagination. We will write "Thank you" for all of the things we want; whether it's money, abundance, love, happiness, health, etc. We will thank God or The Universe for giving it to us, because the truth is, it is already ours! We just need to vibrate on the same level in order to attract our desires. When writing these phrases, think to yourself "My current thoughts are creating my future life." These can be repeated on a daily basis or you can switch them up based on what you need that day.

Make sure to write everything in a positive way. If you feel that you are lacking in some area of your life, rewrite it the same way you'd like to rewrite that area of your life.

Creating Habit

Make sure to reread these phrases and take a moment to breathe them in, believe them and refocus your attention on the words you've written down rather than your past/current thoughts/feelings on the subject.

Remember, it is impossible to be negative when you are grateful. Look for the positives, they are there. The more you see, the sooner the negatives will disappear.

At the beginning and end of each week, there will be prompts to further fuel your progress and help you achieve the vibration you need, to achieve the results you want!

Tips for Journaling:

I've found that starting my morning with this journal helps keep my mind clear and positive throughout the day, so I recommend filling out your journal entry every morning when you first wake up. The prompts at the beginning and end of each week can be filled out at night.

Dedicating 10-30 minutes a day will truly change your life - so don't make excuses. Instead, make the time. Every day, we will start with a thankful mind. You'll see each day has a thankful prompt - say this out loud if you can, or in your head if you're not comfortable. I recommend finding a spot outside on warmer days and a spot near a window on colder days - natural light is always helpful!

Meditation & Visualization

Following each daily entry, you'll be prompted to take a few minutes to yourself to take it all in. If you can, close your eyes and breathe.

Start by focusing on the things you wrote down - truly believe in those words, focus on the fruition of every 'Thank you' you've written down. See it physically come to life, picture it in your mind. How do you feel? Feel the excitement, the happiness, feel every positive emotion you can as you vividly imagine your perfect life.

Finally, focus on the sound of your breath and how your body moves with every inhale and exhale for a few moments. Feel the calmness. Feel the revitalization.

As you continue this process on a daily basis, you are starting to plant seeds into your subconscious mind. The more you believe and feel what you are saying, the faster the seeds you plant will grow. When you can envision the outcome of what you're hoping for, as if it has already happened, your conscious mind will start to believe it and relay the information to your subconscious mind. Your subconscious mind turns these thoughts into feelings and your vibration makes them reality!

Your Truth

Who are you no longer willing to be? Where are you no longer willing to be?

_____

_____

_____

_____

_____

_____

_____

_____

_____

_____

_____

_____

_____

Your Truth

Extra space provided if needed...

_____

_____

_____

_____

_____

_____

_____

_____

_____

_____

_____

_____

Your Truth

In order to move forward we need to know what we want. We just established what we no longer want - who and where we no longer want to be. Now, let's focus on what we do want - who do we want to be, where do we want to go?

Sometimes, we're so worried about the "how" that we forget to focus on what we really want. Instead, we're so focused on all the ways we can't have what we want or how impossible it is to get what we want that we give up on our hopes/dreams without ever even trying to pursue them. It's because we've already convinced ourselves in our minds that it's not possible. We forget however, that possibility is relative. What is possible to you may not be possible to someone else and vice versa - and why is that? What makes something possible for me and not for you?

I'll tell you - it starts with your mind. If you've automatically decided a dream or goal you have is not possible in your mind, then you've already made it impossible - because you've essentially already given up on it. But I'm here to remind you that truly ANYTHING is possible. Look around the world today, how many people are living a life you think is impossible? It's possible for them, so that alone means it is in fact possible!

Now, take a few moments to write about where you want to be and who you want to be **without limits**! Let your imagination wander and write down all that comes to mind. If any fears and doubts creep up, remind yourself that anything is possible and all you're doing right now is writing your hopes and dreams anyway, there's no real pressure.

Your Truth

Who are you?

(Answer this question in the present tense - based on who you want to be. Are you happy? Successful? Excited? Driven? In love with life? The answer is - yes, whether you think so or not in this moment, you have the ability to be all of these things and more! Write it down: I am strong, confident, happy, passionate etc..)

_____

_____

_____

_____

_____

Where are you?

(Answer this question instead - where do you want to be? What do you want to have? Answer in the present tense as if this is already yours)

_____

_____

_____

_____

_____

In a world filled with so much noise, it's easy to get lost, to get frustrated, and overwhelmed. However, everything we need is already within us. We just need to get rid of the outside noise. The same noise that tells us what we are not, where we are not, or who we are not. That is all outside noise.

Who we are - is up to us.
Where we are - is up to us.

Your Truth

Up until this point, you may have had a negative view on yourself. We are no longer going to accept that view. From now on, we know that everything we say to ourselves or about ourselves manifests into reality. For that reason alone, whether we believe it or not in this moment, we will only speak highly of ourselves and to ourselves. Make that decision right now, whether you believe this or not, make the decision to speak only positively when it comes to yourself.

Repeat the affirmations below:

I am strong
I am smart
I am an abundance magnet
I am wealth personified
I am happiness personified
I am success personified
I am love personified
I am light personified
I am healthy
I am powerful
I am worthy

These are just a few affirmations you should be telling yourself daily. After all, you truly are all of these things and more. Eventually, the more you tell yourself, the more you will believe. Thus, you will reprogram your subconscious mind, so that you no longer need to tell yourself, you will just know!

Your Truth

Once you know you are all of these things, you have mastered your mind and therefore will attract all that you want with all that you already are. The key to attraction is gratitude - when you're thankful for what you have, more comes to you.

This journal was intended to help you rediscover what already exists within you. It was created to bring you back to life - the life made for you, by you. Through gratitude, positivity and repetition, you will reprogram your mind to it's natural state - love, light and abundance.

"We become what we want to be by consistently being what we want to become each day."
- Richard G. Scott

This is the second time you are seeing that quote because this is what it is all about.

Finally, I recommend re-reading your journal entry every night before going to sleep. If you can, take a moment to also think about one great thing that happened to you during the day. As you get ready to sleep, close your eyes and think about all of the positive things you are grateful for and all of the positive things to come. With your eyes closed, imagine your perfect life. Focus on your breath, your natural breathing and drift off to sleep in happiness. Remember your thoughts become things and we always have a reason to be happy!

The following three pages contain an example journal entry for the beginning of the week and the daily entries that follow.

Week I - Example Journal Entry

My main goal for this week is...

To complete this journal on a daily basis and make a conscious effort to think positively, and shift my attention from doubts and worries to possibilities. I will keep a positive attitude and be a light in my own life and the lives of those around me.

I am achieving my goal by...

I am achieving my goal by sticking to this morning ritual and completing this journal daily as well as doing things that nourish my mind, body and soul, like reading, walking, meditating and getting daily sun.

Words of Affirmation

I Am abundance personified

I Am divine

I Am capable of achieving all of my dreams

I Am strong, healthy and happy

I Am completely healed, physically, mentally and emotionally

Morning Prompt: *Thank you for waking me up to a new, incredible day*
(read this out loud or say it in your head)

I am truly grateful for _____ (because)

1. I am truly grateful for my health because it allows me to engage in daily activities with vitality, fostering a sense of well-being and accomplishment.

2. I am truly grateful for the changing seasons because they remind me of the cyclical nature of life and offer a constant source of wonder and beauty.

3. I am truly grateful for the friendships in my life because they bring joy, laughter, and a sense of belonging, enriching my journey with shared experiences and support.

4. I am truly grateful for the lessons learned from challenges because they have been catalysts for personal development and resilience.

5. I am truly grateful for the simple pleasures of daily life, such as a warm cup of coffee or a beautiful sunset, as they bring moments of joy and mindfulness.

Today I am letting go of..

Today I am letting go of any negative thoughts or limiting beliefs. I will no longer speak down to myself or worry. I am all that I believe myself to be and so I will only look at what I want to be. All that I want is already mine.

Date: __/__/__

Rephrase negative thoughts/habits I have into positive Thank You's

Let's reprogram our mind, by reprogramming our thoughts!

1. Thank you for the chance to appreciate and strengthen my connection with myself.

2. Thank you for the excitement and possibilities that the future holds, allowing me to shape my own journey.

3. Thank you for the awareness and the chance to prioritize my well-being, making choices that promote a healthy lifestyle.

4. Thank you for the flexibility and adaptability that allow me to navigate unexpected changes with resilience and grace.

5. Thank you for the motivation to set higher standards and strive for continuous improvement in my personal growth.

"Every thought of yours is a real thing - a force" -Prentice Mulford

Thoughts become things! Before we can begin manifesting our reality, we must learn to reprogram our thoughts. After all, manifesting is thinking (thoughts become things). The reason people don't have what they want is because they are constantly focused on just that - what they **don't** have. If we reprogram our mind to be grateful for what we **do** have and turn those negative thoughts into positive ones, we will begin to think of what we **do** have and what we **do** want, rather than the opposite. That is when life begins to change - opportunity enters, abundance fills our lives and we become who we are meant to be.

Start Today

You now have a glimpse of the journey you are about to embark on. At the beginning of each week, there will be an exercise for you to complete. Similarly, at the end of each week, there will be another exercise for you to complete. For this reason, I recommend setting aside some extra time at the beginning and end of each week to really focus on the questions being asked of you. Take your time and answer thoughtfully.

Start today. Week 1 begins on the next page.

May this journal bring you peace, love, health, and happiness as you watch all of your desires come to life!

Welcome to My Positive Mind!

Week 1 will be dedicated to Dreams & Desires

Use the next week to focus on everything you are grateful for about yourself! Your mind, your body, your strengths, your spirit, your energy, etc.

Remember, you are one of a kind. You were perfectly made and there is no one else like you! Your power is unique to you and everything you need is already in you.

Dreams & Desires

Make a list of what you really want in all areas of your life. I've outlined a few areas, but feel free to add or remove any area based on what is important to you. Get specific and clear on what you want in each area. Don't worry about how you are going to achieve what you want, just list exactly what it is you want!
Think of this as "My Millionaire Life" if you weren't worried about money, work, societal expectations, family pressures or anything else you think is getting in the way - what would your life look like? What do you want out of life? Do you want a mansion or 5 different apartments around the world, or both? Do you want to be the CEO of a company or a stay-at-home mom or dad? Nothing is off limits - write out your vision. Start with what you'd like right now in each area of your life and continue with what you envision long term. The more detailed you are, the better! The purpose is to paint a picture of your next-level self aka the future you. Let's get crystal clear.

- Health & Well-Being
- Physical
- Mental
- Relationship
- Career
- Finances
- Social Life
- Spiritual Life

The next few pages have been left blank intentionally for you to fill out your 'Millionaire Life'.

This page was left blank intentionally to continue your list if needed

This page was left blank intentionally to continue your list if needed

This page was left blank intentionally to continue your list if needed

This page was left blank intentionally to continue your list if needed

This page was left blank intentionally to continue your list if needed

This page was left blank intentionally to continue your list if needed

"You don't always need a plan. Sometimes you just need to breathe, trust, let go and see what happens."
-Mandy Hale

Week I

My main goal for this week is...

_____

_____

_____

_____

_____

I am achieving my goal by...

_____

_____

_____

_____

_____

Words of Affirmation

I Am _____

I Am _____

I Am _____

I Am _____

I Am _____

Date: __/__/__

I am truly grateful for _____ (because)

1. _____
_____
_____
_____

2. _____
_____
_____
_____

3. _____
_____
_____
_____

4. _____
_____
_____
_____

5. _____
_____
_____
_____

Today I am letting go of..

_____
_____
_____
_____

Date: __/__/__

Rephrase negative thoughts/habits I have into positive Thank You's

Let's reprogram our mind, by reprogramming our thoughts!

1. _____
_____
_____
_____

2. _____
_____
_____
_____

3. _____
_____
_____
_____

4. _____
_____
_____
_____

5. _____
_____
_____
_____

"Every thought of yours is a real thing - a force" -Prentice Mulford

Thoughts become things! Before we can begin manifesting our reality, we must learn to reprogram our thoughts. After all, manifesting is thinking (thoughts become things). The reason people don't have what they want is because they are constantly focused on just that - what they **don't** have. If we reprogram our mind to be grateful for what we **do** have and turn those negative thoughts into positive ones, we will begin to think of what we **do** have and what we **do** want, rather than the opposite. That is when life begins to change - opportunity enters, abundance fills our lives and we become who we are meant to be.

Meditation & Visualization

Following each daily entry, you'll be prompted to take a few minutes to yourself to take it all in. If you can, close your eyes and breathe.

Start by focusing on the things you wrote down - truly believe in those words, focus on the fruition of every 'Thank you' you've written down. See it physically come to life, picture it in your mind. How do you feel? Feel the excitement, the happiness, feel every positive emotion you can as you vividly imagine your perfect life.

Finally, focus on the sound of your breath and how your body moves with every inhale and exhale for a few moments. Feel the calmness. Feel the revitalization.

As you continue this process on a daily basis, you are starting to plant seeds into your subconscious mind. The more you believe and feel what you are saying, the faster the seeds you plant will grow. When you can envision the outcome of what you're hoping for, as if it has already happened, your conscious mind will start to believe it and relay the information to your subconscious mind. Your subconscious mind turns these thoughts into a reality!

"Nothing is impossible.
The word itself says
'I'm possible!'"
-Audrey Hepburn

Date: __/__/__

Morning Prompt: *Thank you for waking me up to a new, incredible day*
(read this out loud or say it in your head)

I am truly grateful for _____ (because)

1. _____
_____
_____
_____

2. _____
_____
_____
_____

3. _____
_____
_____
_____

4. _____
_____
_____
_____

5. _____
_____
_____
_____

Today I am letting go of..

_____
_____
_____
_____

Date: __/__/__

Rephrase negative thoughts/habits I have into positive Thank You's

Let's reprogram our mind, by reprogramming our thoughts!

1._____
_____
_____
_____

2._____
_____
_____
_____

3._____
_____
_____
_____

4._____
_____
_____
_____

5._____
_____
_____
_____

"Every thought of yours is a real thing - a force" -Prentice Mulford

Thoughts become things! Before we can begin manifesting our reality, we must learn to reprogram our thoughts. After all, manifesting is thinking (thoughts become things). The reason people don't have what they want is because they are constantly focused on just that - what they **don't** have. If we reprogram our mind to be grateful for what we **do** have and turn those negative thoughts into positive ones, we will begin to think of what we **do** have and what we **do** want, rather than the opposite. That is when life begins to change - opportunity enters, abundance fills our lives and we become who we are meant to be.

"Not having the best situation, but seeing the best in your situation is the key to happiness."
-Marie Forleo

Morning Prompt: *Thank you for waking me up to a new, incredible day*
(read this out loud or say it in your head)

I am truly grateful for _____ (because)

1. _____
_____
_____
_____

2. _____
_____
_____
_____

3. _____
_____
_____
_____

4. _____
_____
_____
_____

5. _____
_____
_____
_____

Today I am letting go of..

_____
_____
_____
_____

Date: __/__/__

Rephrase negative thoughts/habits I have into positive Thank You's

Let's reprogram our mind, by reprogramming our thoughts!

1._____

_____

_____

_____

2._____

_____

_____

_____

3._____

_____

_____

_____

4._____

_____

_____

_____

5._____

_____

_____

_____

"Every thought of yours is a real thing - a force" -Prentice Mulford

Thoughts become things! Before we can begin manifesting our reality, we must learn to reprogram our thoughts. After all, manifesting is thinking (thoughts become things). The reason people don't have what they want is because they are constantly focused on just that - what they **don't** have. If we reprogram our mind to be grateful for what we **do** have and turn those negative thoughts into positive ones, we will begin to think of what we **do** have and what we **do** want, rather than the opposite. That is when life begins to change - opportunity enters, abundance fills our lives and we become who we are meant to be.

"Belief creates
the actual fact."
-William James

Date: __/__/__

I am truly grateful for _____ (because)

1. _____
_____
_____
_____

2. _____
_____
_____
_____

3. _____
_____
_____
_____

4. _____
_____
_____
_____

5. _____
_____
_____
_____

Today I am letting go of..

_____
_____
_____
_____

Date: __/__/__

Rephrase negative thoughts/habits I have into positive Thank You's

Let's reprogram our mind, by reprogramming our thoughts!

1. _____
   _____
   _____
   _____

2. _____
   _____
   _____
   _____

3. _____
   _____
   _____
   _____

4. _____
   _____
   _____
   _____

5. _____
   _____
   _____
   _____

"Every thought of yours is a real thing - a force" -Prentice Mulford

Thoughts become things! Before we can begin manifesting our reality, we must learn to reprogram our thoughts. After all, manifesting is thinking (thoughts become things). The reason people don't have what they want is because they are constantly focused on just that - what they **don't** have. If we reprogram our mind to be grateful for what we **do** have and turn those negative thoughts into positive ones, we will begin to think of what we **do** have and what we **do** want, rather than the opposite. That is when life begins to change - opportunity enters, abundance fills our lives and we become who we are meant to be.

"Happiness is when what you think, what you say, and what you do are in harmony."
-Mahatma Gandhi

Date: __/__/__

I am truly grateful for _____ (because)

1. _____
   _____
   _____
   _____

2. _____
   _____
   _____
   _____

3. _____
   _____
   _____
   _____

4. _____
   _____
   _____
   _____

5. _____
   _____
   _____
   _____

Today I am letting go of..

_____
_____
_____
_____

Date: __/__/__

Rephrase negative thoughts/habits I have into positive Thank You's

Let's reprogram our mind, by reprogramming our thoughts!

1. _____
   _____
   _____
   _____

2. _____
   _____
   _____
   _____

3. _____
   _____
   _____
   _____

4. _____
   _____
   _____
   _____

5. _____
   _____
   _____
   _____

"Every thought of yours is a real thing - a force" -Prentice Mulford

Thoughts become things! Before we can begin manifesting our reality, we must learn to reprogram our thoughts. After all, manifesting is thinking (thoughts become things). The reason people don't have what they want is because they are constantly focused on just that - what they **don't** have. If we reprogram our mind to be grateful for what we **do** have and turn those negative thoughts into positive ones, we will begin to think of what we **do** have and what we **do** want, rather than the opposite. That is when life begins to change - opportunity enters, abundance fills our lives and we become who we are meant to be.

"When you are joyful, when you say yes to life and have fun and project positivity all around you, you become a sun in the center of every constellation, and people want to be near you."
-Shannon L. Alder

Date: __/__/__

I am truly grateful for _____ (because)

1. _____
   _____
   _____
   _____

2. _____
   _____
   _____
   _____

3. _____
   _____
   _____
   _____

4. _____
   _____
   _____
   _____

5. _____
   _____
   _____
   _____

Today I am letting go of..

_____
_____
_____
_____

Date: __/__/__

Rephrase negative thoughts/habits I have into positive Thank You's

Let's reprogram our mind, by reprogramming our thoughts!

1. _____
   _____
   _____
   _____

2. _____
   _____
   _____
   _____

3. _____
   _____
   _____
   _____

4. _____
   _____
   _____
   _____

5. _____
   _____
   _____
   _____

"Every thought of yours is a real thing - a force" -Prentice Mulford

Thoughts become things! Before we can begin manifesting our reality, we must learn to reprogram our thoughts. After all, manifesting is thinking (thoughts become things). The reason people don't have what they want is because they are constantly focused on just that - what they **don't** have. If we reprogram our mind to be grateful for what we **do** have and turn those negative thoughts into positive ones, we will begin to think of what we **do** have and what we **do** want, rather than the opposite. That is when life begins to change - opportunity enters, abundance fills our lives and we become who we are meant to be.

"Be positive. Your mind is more powerful than you think. What is down in the well comes up in the bucket. Fill yourself with positive things."
-Tony Dungy

Date: __/__/__

I am truly grateful for _____ (because)

1. _____
   _____
   _____
   _____

2. _____
   _____
   _____
   _____

3. _____
   _____
   _____
   _____

4. _____
   _____
   _____
   _____

5. _____
   _____
   _____
   _____

Today I am letting go of..

_____
_____
_____
_____

Date: __/__/__

Rephrase negative thoughts/habits I have into positive Thank You's

Let's reprogram our mind, by reprogramming our thoughts!

1._____
_____
_____
_____

2._____
_____
_____
_____

3._____
_____
_____
_____

4._____
_____
_____
_____

5._____
_____
_____
_____

"Every thought of yours is a real thing - a force" -Prentice Mulford

Thoughts become things! Before we can begin manifesting our reality, we must learn to reprogram our thoughts. After all, manifesting is thinking (thoughts become things). The reason people don't have what they want is because they are constantly focused on just that - what they **don't** have. If we reprogram our mind to be grateful for what we **do** have and turn those negative thoughts into positive ones, we will begin to think of what we **do** have and what we **do** want, rather than the opposite. That is when life begins to change - opportunity enters, abundance fills our lives and we become who we are meant to be.

Dreams & Desires

Go back to your list from the beginning of this week and label each area out of 10. For example, for 'Health' - if you're struggling with your health, you could label Health as a 5/10. Based on your labels, which areas of your life have the lowest score? List each area below in order of lowest to highest score:

The lowest scored areas will get priority (if that is where you want to focus your attention and gratitude) in order to transform these areas. The purpose here is to choose the top 3 areas of your life that you want to prioritize and work on first. Once you decide what these three areas are, list them below then follow the prompts:

- Area of Focus 1:

- Area of Focus 2:

- Area of Focus 3:

Dreams & Desires

Under each area, list your top 3 goals for that area

Area of Focus: _____

_____

_____

_____

_____

Area of Focus: _____

_____

_____

_____

_____

Area of Focus: _____

_____

_____

_____

_____

Dreams & Desires

Now reword these goals, as if they have already been achieved. For example, "I am perfectly healthy" or "All of my debt has been paid off and I am now saving $1K a week!"

Area of Focus:

_____
_____
_____
_____

Area of Focus:

_____
_____
_____
_____

Area of Focus:

_____
_____
_____
_____

Reread your list and before each statement say "I am so thankful that..." For example, "I am so thankful that I am perfectly healthy." or "I am so thankful that all of my debt has been paid off and I can now save $1K a week!" Visualize it until you can physically feel it!

"Gratitude can transform common days into thanksgivings, turn routine jobs into joy, and change ordinary opportunities into blessings."
—William Arthur Ward

"The greatest discovery of all time is that a person can change his future by merely changing his attitude."
-Oprah Winfrey

Week 2 will be dedicated to Understanding your Current Results in order to change your Future

Use the next week to focus on how far you've come! Whether you are where you wanted to be or not, you started somewhere. If nothing else, focus on the little steps that got you here, to this journal and journey.

Be grateful for all of the lessons along the way and all of the lessons to come. Remember, you attract what you are in harmonious vibration with!

Understanding
Your Current Results

When reviewing our current results, it's important to remember that "thoughts become things". Our current results are based on our previous thoughts!

Take a few moments to review your current results, specifically in the areas of your life that you have been focusing on improving. What have your thoughts about this area been prior to this journal? Or maybe, subconsciously, you still hold similar thoughts.

Here's an example: Up until this point, I've viewed money as difficult to make. I've viewed it as the cause of most of the stress in my life and as something I must work extremely hard for in order to receive. As a result, my bank account reflects this and I do not have enough money for all that I want or need.

Pay attention to the negative cycle that arises due to these thoughts. My thoughts on money have manifested into the physical world (in my bank account) and now I am focused on my current results - the negative results in my bank account. I look at my bank account everyday and focus on the **lack** of money. This lack of money causes me more stress and further instills my initial thoughts on how difficult it is to make money, etc. These negative thoughts will continue to manifest in physical form and as a result, my future results will continue to reflect this lack of money. It's a cycle because my thoughts and feelings are staying the same and I am vibrating on the same frequency!

Understanding
Your Current Results

Previous thoughts:
- Money is difficult to make
- I will never have enough money
- Money causes stress and anxiety
- I can't afford that
- I don't have enough money
- I must work hard to make money
- I hate money

Current Results
Physical Manifestation of Thoughts
- My bank account reflects my thoughts
- I don't make enough money
- I didn't get the raise I wanted
- I work hard everyday and feel like my work goes unnoticed
- My credit card bills are high
- I am stressing about my bills because I don't know how I will pay them

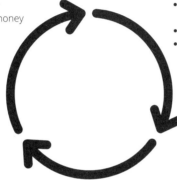

Living Through My Senses (instead of choosing new thoughts)
- Looking at my bank account everyday and the lack of money further reinforces my previous thoughts (keeping my vibration the same)
- Stressing about my bills and how I will pay them further reinforces my previous thoughts (keeping my vibration the same)
- Showing up to work everyday, unhappy and ungrateful for my job further reinforces my previous thoughts (keeping my vibration the same)

Here's where things get promising. Most people don't realize that they are going through life without thinking, like in the example above. Instead of actually thinking, I am just living through my senses, the way I have been programmed to live. I focus on my present results which control my thinking and therefore create more of the same results.

In order to change our results, we must remember that thoughts become things and we have the power to choose our thoughts.

Understanding
Your Current Results

I have the power to choose! If I decide today to stop focusing on the lack of money, the physical amount in my bank account and instead decide that I will have a new number in my bank account - my results *must* change - because thoughts become things! Rather than allowing my senses and surroundings (current bank account numbers) control my thinking - I will use my mind to control and create my future. I will build the idea and get emotionally involved with it - I will feel it and believe it to life.

Choose your thoughts: I now choose to view money as easy to make. I believe that I am abundant and that money comes to me easily. I believe that having money is my birthright and every dollar I spend comes back to me times 10.

These are a few examples of how I am choosing thoughts that align with the future results I want to attract. I am choosing to think of what I **do** want and I am deciding today that I will no longer allow the outside control or limit my thinking. I will vibrate at a higher frequency!

Reviewing
Your Current Results

What are your current results? (Answer based on the areas of your life that you'd like to change. Be honest and write down your results in a 'matter of fact' list form, do not include your thoughts/feelings surrounding these results)

_____
_____
_____
_____
_____
_____
_____
_____
_____
_____
_____
_____
_____
_____
_____
_____
_____
_____
_____
_____
_____
_____
_____

Reviewing
Your Current Results

What thoughts have contributed to your current results? (What do you believe to be true about yourself? What are some thoughts you have around these areas of your life? What were you taught growing up? For example, a lot of people believe/say "Money is not important" - the truth is - money is important and you should have as much as you want to do with what you want.) Write down your beliefs below:

_____
_____
_____
_____
_____
_____
_____
_____
_____
_____
_____
_____
_____
_____
_____
_____
_____
_____
_____
_____

This page was left blank intentionally to continue your list if needed

Changing
Your Future Results

When you make a decision - the universe works towards that decision.

We live on a floating planet in the middle of space - ANYTHING is truly possible. Start to take notice of when you tell yourself that something is impossible. Laugh at the thought of it being impossible. Laughing will allow you to change your state (your vibration) and get rid of resistance. It will also help you to expand your realm of possibility.

Let's rewrite our thoughts (based on the future we want). Write down these new thoughts in the present moment - if you'd like, they can also be affirmations written as "I am wealthy, I make money easily, I am perfectly healthy, My body heals quickly and with ease, etc." You get to CHOOSE your thoughts, so write down your new beliefs, as these will be the beliefs we focus on going forward.

_____

_____

_____

_____

_____

_____

_____

_____

_____

This page was left blank intentionally to continue your list if needed

Changing
Your Future Results

What does your future look like, if you could choose? Take a few minutes to visualize it. The truth is, we want things because of the way they make us feel. Most of us just want to feel happy. So, rather than forming attachments to the things, we should form attachments to the feelings.

Take time everyday to visualize your future self and **feel** the excitement and happiness of your wishes coming to fruition. Remind yourself " I don't know how, when or where, but I am excited for _____, I know it's going to happen!" Feeling is the vibration and our goal is to live in harmonious vibration with the things we want to attract.

Now that you've spent some time thinking about your future life and future self - what is he/she doing? Are they working out 3-4 times a week? Are they drinking green smoothies first thing in the morning? Are they attending networking events? Are they waking up at 6am every morning? etc. What actions can you take right now that your future self would be taking? Write them down and make an effort to start today.

This page was left blank intentionally to continue your list if needed

Week II

My main goal for this week is...

_____

_____

_____

_____

_____

I am achieving my goal by...

_____

_____

_____

_____

Words of Affirmation

I Am _____

I Am _____

I Am _____

I Am _____

I Am _____

Date: __/__/__

Morning Prompt: *Thank you for waking me up to a new, incredible day*
(read this out loud or say it in your head)

I am truly grateful for _____ (because)

1. _____
   _____
   _____
   _____

2. _____
   _____
   _____
   _____

3. _____
   _____
   _____
   _____

4. _____
   _____
   _____
   _____

5. _____
   _____
   _____
   _____

Today I am letting go of..

_____
_____
_____
_____

Date: __/__/__

Rephrase negative thoughts/habits I have into positive Thank You's

Let's reprogram our mind, by reprogramming our thoughts!

1._____
_____
_____
_____

2._____
_____
_____
_____

3._____
_____
_____
_____

4._____
_____
_____
_____

5._____
_____
_____
_____

"Every thought of yours is a real thing - a force" -Prentice Mulford

Thoughts become things! Before we can begin manifesting our reality, we must learn to reprogram our thoughts. After all, manifesting is thinking (thoughts become things). The reason people don't have what they want is because they are constantly focused on just that - what they **don't** have. If we reprogram our mind to be grateful for what we **do** have and turn those negative thoughts into positive ones, we will begin to think of what we **do** have and what we **do** want, rather than the opposite. That is when life begins to change - opportunity enters, abundance fills our lives and we become who we are meant to be.

Meditation & Visualization

Following each daily entry, you'll be prompted to take a few minutes to yourself to take it all in. If you can, close your eyes and breathe.

Start by focusing on the things you wrote down - truly believe in those words, focus on the fruition of every 'Thank you' you've written down. See it physically come to life, picture it in your mind. How do you feel? Feel the excitement, the happiness, feel every positive emotion you can as you vividly imagine your perfect life.

Finally, focus on the sound of your breath and how your body moves with every inhale and exhale for a few moments. Feel the calmness. Feel the revitalization.

As you continue this process on a daily basis, you are starting to plant seeds into your subconscious mind. The more you believe and feel what you are saying, the faster the seeds you plant will grow. When you can envision the outcome of what you're hoping for, as if it has already happened, your conscious mind will start to believe it and relay the information to your subconscious mind. Your subconscious mind turns these thoughts into a reality!

"Believe you can and you're halfway there."
-Theodore Roosevelt

Date: __/__/__

I am truly grateful for _____ (because)

1. _____
   _____
   _____
   _____

2. _____
   _____
   _____
   _____

3. _____
   _____
   _____
   _____

4. _____
   _____
   _____
   _____

5. _____
   _____
   _____
   _____

Today I am letting go of..

_____
_____
_____
_____

Date: __/__/__

Rephrase negative thoughts/habits I have into positive Thank You's

Let's reprogram our mind, by reprogramming our thoughts!

1. _____
_____
_____
_____

2. _____
_____
_____
_____

3. _____
_____
_____
_____

4. _____
_____
_____
_____

5. _____
_____
_____
_____

"Every thought of yours is a real thing - a force" -Prentice Mulford

Thoughts become things! Before we can begin manifesting our reality, we must learn to reprogram our thoughts. After all, manifesting is thinking (thoughts become things). The reason people don't have what they want is because they are constantly focused on just that - what they **don't** have. If we reprogram our mind to be grateful for what we **do** have and turn those negative thoughts into positive ones, we will begin to think of what we **do** have and what we **do** want, rather than the opposite. That is when life begins to change - opportunity enters, abundance fills our lives and we become who we are meant to be.

"It is never too late to be what you might have been."
-George Eliot

Date: __/__/__

I am truly grateful for _____ (because)

1. _____
   _____
   _____
   _____

2. _____
   _____
   _____
   _____

3. _____
   _____
   _____
   _____

4. _____
   _____
   _____
   _____

5. _____
   _____
   _____
   _____

Today I am letting go of..

_____
_____
_____
_____

Date: __/__/__

Rephrase negative thoughts/habits I have into positive Thank You's

Let's reprogram our mind, by reprogramming our thoughts!

1._____
_____
_____
_____

2._____
_____
_____
_____

3._____
_____
_____
_____

4._____
_____
_____
_____

5._____
_____
_____
_____

"Every thought of yours is a real thing - a force" -Prentice Mulford

Thoughts become things! Before we can begin manifesting our reality, we must learn to reprogram our thoughts. After all, manifesting is thinking (thoughts become things). The reason people don't have what they want is because they are constantly focused on just that - what they **don't** have. If we reprogram our mind to be grateful for what we **do** have and turn those negative thoughts into positive ones, we will begin to think of what we **do** have and what we **do** want, rather than the opposite. That is when life begins to change - opportunity enters, abundance fills our lives and we become who we are meant to be.

"You must find the place inside yourself where nothing is impossible."
-Deepak Chopra

Date: __/__/__

I am truly grateful for _____ (because)

1. _____
   _____
   _____
   _____

2. _____
   _____
   _____
   _____

3. _____
   _____
   _____
   _____

4. _____
   _____
   _____
   _____

5. _____
   _____
   _____
   _____

Today I am letting go of..

_____
_____
_____
_____

Date: __/__/__

Rephrase negative thoughts/habits I have into positive Thank You's

Let's reprogram our mind, by reprogramming our thoughts!

1._____

_____

_____

_____

2._____

_____

_____

_____

3._____

_____

_____

_____

4._____

_____

_____

_____

5._____

_____

_____

_____

"Every thought of yours is a real thing - a force" -Prentice Mulford

Thoughts become things! Before we can begin manifesting our reality, we must learn to reprogram our thoughts. After all, manifesting is thinking (thoughts become things). The reason people don't have what they want is because they are constantly focused on just that - what they **don't** have. If we reprogram our mind to be grateful for what we **do** have and turn those negative thoughts into positive ones, we will begin to think of what we **do** have and what we **do** want, rather than the opposite. That is when life begins to change - opportunity enters, abundance fills our lives and we become who we are meant to be.

"Change yourself – you are in control."
-Mahatma Gandhi

Date: __/__/__

I am truly grateful for _____ (because)

1. _____
   _____
   _____
   _____

2. _____
   _____
   _____
   _____

3. _____
   _____
   _____
   _____

4. _____
   _____
   _____
   _____

5. _____
   _____
   _____
   _____

Today I am letting go of..

_____
_____
_____
_____

Date: __/__/__

Rephrase negative thoughts/habits I have into positive Thank You's

Let's reprogram our mind, by reprogramming our thoughts!

1. _____
   _____
   _____
   _____

2. _____
   _____
   _____
   _____

3. _____
   _____
   _____
   _____

4. _____
   _____
   _____
   _____

5. _____
   _____
   _____
   _____

"Every thought of yours is a real thing - a force" -Prentice Mulford

Thoughts become things! Before we can begin manifesting our reality, we must learn to reprogram our thoughts. After all, manifesting is thinking (thoughts become things). The reason people don't have what they want is because they are constantly focused on just that - what they **don't** have. If we reprogram our mind to be grateful for what we **do** have and turn those negative thoughts into positive ones, we will begin to think of what we **do** have and what we **do** want, rather than the opposite. That is when life begins to change - opportunity enters, abundance fills our lives and we become who we are meant to be.

"Don't be pushed around by the fears in your mind. Be led by the dreams in your heart."
-Roy T. Bennett

Date: __/__/__

Morning Prompt: *Thank you for waking me up to a new, incredible day*
(read this out loud or say it in your head)

I am truly grateful for _____ (because)

1. _____
_____
_____
_____

2. _____
_____
_____
_____

3. _____
_____
_____
_____

4. _____
_____
_____
_____

5. _____
_____
_____
_____

Today I am letting go of..

_____
_____
_____
_____

Date: __/__/__

Rephrase negative thoughts/habits I have into positive Thank You's

Let's reprogram our mind, by reprogramming our thoughts!

1. _____

_____

_____

_____

2. _____

_____

_____

_____

3. _____

_____

_____

_____

4. _____

_____

_____

_____

5. _____

_____

_____

_____

"Every thought of yours is a real thing - a force" -Prentice Mulford

Thoughts become things! Before we can begin manifesting our reality, we must learn to reprogram our thoughts. After all, manifesting is thinking (thoughts become things). The reason people don't have what they want is because they are constantly focused on just that - what they **don't** have. If we reprogram our mind to be grateful for what we **do** have and turn those negative thoughts into positive ones, we will begin to think of what we **do** have and what we **do** want, rather than the opposite. That is when life begins to change - opportunity enters, abundance fills our lives and we become who we are meant to be.

"It's a funny thing about life, once you begin to take note of the things you are grateful for, you begin to lose sight of the things that you lack."
-Germany Kent

Morning Prompt: *Thank you for waking me up to a new, incredible day*
(read this out loud or say it in your head)

I am truly grateful for _____ (because)

1. _____
   _____
   _____
   _____

2. _____
   _____
   _____
   _____

3. _____
   _____
   _____
   _____

4. _____
   _____
   _____
   _____

5. _____
   _____
   _____
   _____

Today I am letting go of..

_____
_____
_____
_____

Date: __/__/__

Rephrase negative thoughts/habits I have into positive Thank You's

Let's reprogram our mind, by reprogramming our thoughts!

1. _____
   _____
   _____
   _____

2. _____
   _____
   _____
   _____

3. _____
   _____
   _____
   _____

4. _____
   _____
   _____
   _____

5. _____
   _____
   _____
   _____

"Every thought of yours is a real thing - a force" -Prentice Mulford

Thoughts become things! Before we can begin manifesting our reality, we must learn to reprogram our thoughts. After all, manifesting is thinking (thoughts become things). The reason people don't have what they want is because they are constantly focused on just that - what they **don't** have. If we reprogram our mind to be grateful for what we **do** have and turn those negative thoughts into positive ones, we will begin to think of what we **do** have and what we **do** want, rather than the opposite. That is when life begins to change - opportunity enters, abundance fills our lives and we become who we are meant to be.

Getting into Alignment

Let's go back to the top 3 goals you listed at the end of last week for each area of your life that you want to prioritize. It's time to get into alignment! Who do you need to become in order to achieve these goals? What actions do you need to take?

Go back and pick one specific goal from each area that you want to focus on acheiving first. Write each one down below:

Goal #1:

_____

Goal #2:

_____

Goal #3:

_____

Now for each goal listed above, write down one action you can take on a daily basis to help you achieve that goal:

Action #1:

_____

Action #2:

_____

Action #3:

_____

Getting into Alignment

"You've got to be before you can do, and do before you can have."
– Zig Ziglar

Getting into alignment essentially means that we need to **be**-come the kind of person we want to be, in order to **do** what we need to do to **have** what we want to have.

This is known as the Be-Do-Have Principal.

So often we approach life in the opposite way, with a Have-Do-Be mindset. We think we need to "have" certain things, like more money or more time, in order to "do" something important to us like start a business or go on a dream vacation, which will then allow us to "be" what we truly want in life (happy). This thought process is actually completely backwards. The truth is we must BE in order to DO and when we DO, then we can HAVE. Remember, we attract who/what we are!

New mindset = New Results

In order to "BE", consider the following questions:
What specific qualities or skills are you going to work on? What are you going to listen to or read to get you in the right mindset? Who will you spend time with?

Being isn't about perfection, it's about intentional, incremental changes and it starts with fueling your mind with the right information. It's about feeling. Being is feeling happy or calm or just present, right here and right now.

Getting into Alignment

For the past 2 weeks, you've been working on **be**ing grateful and positive. You've already started **being**. Everything you want is already yours! You just need to get into alignment.

In the beginning of this journal I asked you two questions: "Who are you?" (who do you want to be?) and "Where are you?" (where do you want to be? what do you want to have?) I asked you to answer these questions in the present tense.

Now, we already know what you want to have (based on the goals you've written down), so it's time to think about this again.

Let's try a quick exercise:

Close your eyes and picture yourself in the future. Imagine that your ideal goals have unfolded and that you've reached a stage that you consider extremely successful. Visualize. Once you've reached this level of success, how would you act? how would you carry yourself? how would you treat others? how much energy would you pour into what it is you do? how content would you feel? how would you help others who are looking to achieve the same goals?

Now ask yourself this: Why not act, feel and carry yourself that way now? If you really think about it, this version of you already exists (it's just energy waiting to move into another form), and the sooner you act like it, the sooner you will align and manifest into physical form!

Getting into Alignment

Answer the following questions in list form:

Who do you need to be? (Calm, organized, happy, excited, motivated, confident, inspiring, etc.)

_____

_____

_____

_____

_____

_____

_____

_____

_____

_____

What do you need to do? (Create Tasks/To-do list, exercise, network, read, journal, listen to podcasts, complete this journal, etc.)

_____

_____

_____

_____

_____

_____

_____

_____

_____

_____

Getting into Alignment

In order to "Be" and "Do" we must carve out the time. Use this page to create your 'Ideal schedule' - create this schedule around your goals. For example, if health is a priority, start your day with a healthy habit. Write in the times on the left side (blank) from the time you wake up to the time you go to sleep and fill in your ideal day.

_____

_____

_____

_____

_____

_____

_____

_____

_____

_____

_____

_____

_____

_____

_____

_____

_____

_____

_____

_____

Getting into Alignment

Based on all you've written down over the last few pages, what are two small, intentional habits you can adopt over the next few weeks to get you closer to your goal?

Examples:

Wake up Time: Let's say you want to start waking up at 6am everyday. In order to turn this into a habit, you'll need to start slow. For example, start by setting your alarm 10 minutes earlier than you currently wake up. Every day or every 2 days, set it 10 minutes earlier, until you are at the 6am time. Eventually, it will become automatic!

Working out: Start by setting aside 10 minutes a day to work out - whether it's a walk, a jog, a stretching session - anything that gets your body moving. 10 minutes a day for 3-4 days, then increase it to 15 or 20 minutes a day. Don't miss a day, even if it's only 10 minutes, DO it. This is how we create habits that will last.

What are 2 habits you are going to stick to from today on? How will you start slowly? Who will you tell to keep you accountable? Use the space below to elaborate:

_____
_____
_____
_____
_____
_____
_____

This page was left blank intentionally to continue your list if needed

"You are what you are and you are where you are because of what has gone into your mind. You change what you are and you change where you are by changing what goes into your mind."
-Zig Ziglar

Week 3 will be dedicated to changing and expanding our realm of possibility so that all we desire is ours!

Use the next week to focus on the fact that you are possible! You are here, now, on this floating rock in the middle of space. If that is possible, why do you limit what else is possible?

The Idea of Impossible

The word impossible literally says "I'm possible" or "I am possible" If you are possible, here on this earth, on this rock floating in the middle of space - what is not possible?

The reason this is titled "The idea of Impossible" is because the word impossible is just that - an idea. It is another thought that you can decide to choose. How many things were impossible before they were possible? They were made possible because of the individuals who **chose** to believe in themselves.

One of the very first quotes in this book states "Whatever the mind can conceive and believe it can achieve." These are some of the most powerful words ever written. They hold the secret of the Universe - thoughts become things! If your thoughts are constantly negative - those thoughts become things, the same way your positive thoughts become things.

Let's go back to the word impossible - every time you hear, think or see this word - I want you to change it to "I am possible". When you change it to this, I want you to realize that the chances of your existence are "impossible" and yet here you are.

You are here for a reason. You are possible for a reason. Impossible is only an idea created in your mind, by your own limiting thoughts and beliefs. Last week we worked on changing our inherent beliefs in order to change our lives. Let's revisit those beliefs, are there any beliefs or dreams that you currently hold that you believe are impossible?

The Idea of Impossible

If so, I want you to take a moment to write down any and all beliefs you have about yourself or the world that you believe are impossible. (Do you believe winning the lotto is impossible? Do you believe meeting the love of your life is impossible? or that it's impossible for you to become a billionaire? or to lose 50lbs?) What is impossible to you? Use the space below to elaborate:

_____
_____
_____
_____
_____
_____
_____
_____
_____
_____
_____
_____
_____
_____
_____
_____
_____
_____
_____
_____
_____
_____
_____
_____
_____

The Idea of Impossible

Now, let's take a look at the list you just made. For each "impossibility" you listed, I want you to think to yourself - has anyone else achieved this? Whether you know them personally or not, has this been achieved before? I want you to place a check mark next to each thing that has already been achieved by someone else and a large question mark next to anything on your list that hasn't already been achieved by someone else.

Let's start with the check marks. Clearly, these things are not impossible, because they have already been achieved. You might be thinking to yourself "well they're impossible for me" - but if someone else has achieved these things, why can't you? What perception or better yet, what limiting beliefs do you still hold? What lies are you telling yourself? I say lies, because the truth is beyond these limiting beliefs. The truth is that you are divinely created, YOU are possible and therefore anything you desire is possible. The only thing keeping you from your desires is the belief you hold that you cannot achieve them. Once you change your perception, you change your life. It's the reason this journal exists, it's the way your life has been changing up until now because of your new perception on gratitude.

For every check mark, I want you to write down your limiting beliefs on the next page. Once you write down each limiting belief, I want you to think to yourself "What if this wasn't true?" Then cross out the limiting belief you listed and rewrite a new belief based on the statement "If this can be achieved by someone else, it can surely be achieved by me. The people who have already achieved this have made it clear this is very possible."

The Idea of Impossible

Example
Limiting belief: I cannot make 1 million dollars
Checkmark thoughts around this belief: Millionaires exist all over the world, in fact, multi-millionaires, billionaires and multi-billionaires exist. Why am I limiting myself with my thoughts, when someone else makes 1 million dollars a day?
New inherent belief: I am a millionaire. Money flows to me easily. I am abundance personified.

Use the space below to list the limiting beliefs you hold, think about what the check mark represents. This thought is not impossible, it's only impossible for you at this moment because you are limiting yourself. Create a new inherent belief to replace your old one.

_____
_____
_____
_____
_____
_____
_____
_____
_____
_____
_____
_____
_____
_____
_____
_____
_____

This page was left blank intentionally to continue your list if needed

The Idea of Impossible

Now for the question marks, if there are any. If you have question marks listed, this is very exciting. This means you have unqiue ideas that do not yet exist. Remember "I am possible".

Every **thing** was first a **thought**. For each question mark, I want you to write down why you think these things are impossible - what is stopping you or holding you back? Do these thoughts align with your higher self? Do they align with the part of you that knows you are destined for more? The part of you that knows and acknowledges that YOU are possible and therefore all things are possible?

Write down why you think these things are impossible and then rephrase those exact thoughts. Thoughts become things - change your thoughts and you too can turn them into things!

_____
_____
_____
_____
_____
_____
_____
_____
_____
_____
_____
_____
_____
_____
_____
_____
_____

This page was left blank intentionally to continue your list if needed

Week III

My main goal for this week is...

_____

_____

_____

_____

I am achieving my goal by...

_____

_____

_____

_____

Words of Affirmation

I Am _____

I Am _____

I Am _____

I Am _____

I Am _____

Date: __/__/__

I am truly grateful for _____ (because)

1. _____
_____
_____
_____

2. _____
_____
_____
_____

3. _____
_____
_____
_____

4. _____
_____
_____
_____

5. _____
_____
_____
_____

Today I am letting go of..

_____
_____
_____
_____

Date: __/__/__

Rephrase negative thoughts/habits I have into positive Thank You's

Let's reprogram our mind, by reprogramming our thoughts!

1._____
_____
_____
_____

2._____
_____
_____
_____

3._____
_____
_____
_____

4._____
_____
_____
_____

5._____
_____
_____
_____

"Every thought of yours is a real thing - a force" -Prentice Mulford

Thoughts become things! Before we can begin manifesting our reality, we must learn to reprogram our thoughts. After all, manifesting is thinking (thoughts become things). The reason people don't have what they want is because they are constantly focused on just that - what they **don't** have. If we reprogram our mind to be grateful for what we **do** have and turn those negative thoughts into positive ones, we will begin to think of what we **do** have and what we **do** want, rather than the opposite. That is when life begins to change - opportunity enters, abundance fills our lives and we become who we are meant to be.

Meditation & Visualization

Following each daily entry, you'll be prompted to take a few minutes to yourself to take it all in. If you can, close your eyes and breathe.

Start by focusing on the things you wrote down - truly believe in those words, focus on the fruition of every 'Thank you' you've written down. See it physically come to life, picture it in your mind. How do you feel? Feel the excitement, the happiness, feel every positive emotion you can as you vividly imagine your perfect life.

Finally, focus on the sound of your breath and how your body moves with every inhale and exhale for a few moments. Feel the calmness. Feel the revitalization.

As you continue this process on a daily basis, you are starting to plant seeds into your subconscious mind. The more you believe and feel what you are saying, the faster the seeds you plant will grow. When you can envision the outcome of what you're hoping for, as if it has already happened, your conscious mind will start to believe it and relay the information to your subconscious mind. Your subconscious mind turns these thoughts into a reality!

"Things work out best for those who make the best of how things work out."
-John Wooden

Date: __/__/__

I am truly grateful for _____ (because)

1. _____
_____
_____
_____

2. _____
_____
_____
_____

3. _____
_____
_____
_____

4. _____
_____
_____
_____

5. _____
_____
_____
_____

Today I am letting go of..

_____
_____
_____
_____

Date: __/__/__

Rephrase negative thoughts/habits I have into positive Thank You's

Let's reprogram our mind, by reprogramming our thoughts!

1._____
_____
_____
_____

2._____
_____
_____
_____

3._____
_____
_____
_____

4._____
_____
_____
_____

5._____
_____
_____
_____

"Every thought of yours is a real thing - a force" -Prentice Mulford

Thoughts become things! Before we can begin manifesting our reality, we must learn to reprogram our thoughts. After all, manifesting is thinking (thoughts become things). The reason people don't have what they want is because they are constantly focused on just that - what they **don't** have. If we reprogram our mind to be grateful for what we **do** have and turn those negative thoughts into positive ones, we will begin to think of what we **do** have and what we **do** want, rather than the opposite. That is when life begins to change - opportunity enters, abundance fills our lives and we become who we are meant to be.

"The starting point of all achievement is desire."
-Napoleon Hill

Date: __/__/__

I am truly grateful for _____ (because)

1. _____
_____
_____
_____

2. _____
_____
_____
_____

3. _____
_____
_____
_____

4. _____
_____
_____
_____

5. _____
_____
_____
_____

Today I am letting go of..

_____
_____
_____
_____

Date: __/__/__

Rephrase negative thoughts/habits I have into positive Thank You's

Let's reprogram our mind, by reprogramming our thoughts!

1. _____
_____
_____
_____

2. _____
_____
_____
_____

3. _____
_____
_____
_____

4. _____
_____
_____
_____

5. _____
_____
_____
_____

"Every thought of yours is a real thing - a force" -Prentice Mulford

Thoughts become things! Before we can begin manifesting our reality, we must learn to reprogram our thoughts. After all, manifesting is thinking (thoughts become things). The reason people don't have what they want is because they are constantly focused on just that - what they **don't** have. If we reprogram our mind to be grateful for what we **do** have and turn those negative thoughts into positive ones, we will begin to think of what we **do** have and what we **do** want, rather than the opposite. That is when life begins to change - opportunity enters, abundance fills our lives and we become who we are meant to be.

"Motivation is what gets you started. Habit is what keeps you going."
-Jim Ryun

Date: __/__/__

Morning Prompt: *Thank you for waking me up to a new, incredible day*
(read this out loud or say it in your head)

I am truly grateful for _____ (because)

1. _____

_____

_____

_____

2. _____

_____

_____

_____

3. _____

_____

_____

_____

4. _____

_____

_____

_____

5. _____

_____

_____

_____

Today I am letting go of..

_____

_____

_____

_____

Date: __/__/__

Rephrase negative thoughts/habits I have into positive Thank You's

Let's reprogram our mind, by reprogramming our thoughts!

1. _____

   _____

   _____

   _____

2. _____

   _____

   _____

   _____

3. _____

   _____

   _____

   _____

4. _____

   _____

   _____

   _____

5. _____

   _____

   _____

   _____

"Every thought of yours is a real thing - a force" -Prentice Mulford

Thoughts become things! Before we can begin manifesting our reality, we must learn to reprogram our thoughts. After all, manifesting is thinking (thoughts become things). The reason people don't have what they want is because they are constantly focused on just that - what they **don't** have. If we reprogram our mind to be grateful for what we **do** have and turn those negative thoughts into positive ones, we will begin to think of what we **do** have and what we **do** want, rather than the opposite. That is when life begins to change - opportunity enters, abundance fills our lives and we become who we are meant to be.

"Success is the sum of small efforts, repeated day-in and day-out."
-Robert Collier

Date: __/__/__

I am truly grateful for _____ (because)

1. _____
_____
_____
_____

2. _____
_____
_____
_____

3. _____
_____
_____
_____

4. _____
_____
_____
_____

5. _____
_____
_____
_____

Today I am letting go of..

_____
_____
_____
_____

Date: __/__/__

Rephrase negative thoughts/habits I have into positive Thank You's

Let's reprogram our mind, by reprogramming our thoughts!

1. _____
   _____
   _____
   _____

2. _____
   _____
   _____
   _____

3. _____
   _____
   _____
   _____

4. _____
   _____
   _____
   _____

5. _____
   _____
   _____
   _____

"Every thought of yours is a real thing - a force" -Prentice Mulford

Thoughts become things! Before we can begin manifesting our reality, we must learn to reprogram our thoughts. After all, manifesting is thinking (thoughts become things). The reason people don't have what they want is because they are constantly focused on just that - what they **don't** have. If we reprogram our mind to be grateful for what we **do** have and turn those negative thoughts into positive ones, we will begin to think of what we **do** have and what we **do** want, rather than the opposite. That is when life begins to change - opportunity enters, abundance fills our lives and we become who we are meant to be.

"Do not allow negative thoughts to enter your mind for they are weeds that strangle confidence."
-Bruce Lee

Date: __/__/__

Morning Prompt: *Thank you for waking me up to a new, incredible day*
(read this out loud or say it in your head)

I am truly grateful for _____ (because)

1. _____
_____
_____
_____

2. _____
_____
_____
_____

3. _____
_____
_____
_____

4. _____
_____
_____
_____

5. _____
_____
_____
_____

Today I am letting go of..

_____
_____
_____
_____

Date: __/__/__

Rephrase negative thoughts/habits I have into positive Thank You's

Let's reprogram our mind, by reprogramming our thoughts!

1. _____
   _____
   _____
   _____

2. _____
   _____
   _____
   _____

3. _____
   _____
   _____
   _____

4. _____
   _____
   _____
   _____

5. _____
   _____
   _____
   _____

"Every thought of yours is a real thing - a force" -Prentice Mulford

Thoughts become things! Before we can begin manifesting our reality, we must learn to reprogram our thoughts. After all, manifesting is thinking (thoughts become things). The reason people don't have what they want is because they are constantly focused on just that - what they **don't** have. If we reprogram our mind to be grateful for what we **do** have and turn those negative thoughts into positive ones, we will begin to think of what we **do** have and what we **do** want, rather than the opposite. That is when life begins to change - opportunity enters, abundance fills our lives and we become who we are meant to be.

"If you put negative thoughts into your mind, you're going to get negative results. It's just as true that if you put positive thoughts in your mind, you will be a recipient of positive results."
-Lou Holtz

Date: __/__/__

I am truly grateful for _____ (because)

1. _____
_____
_____
_____

2. _____
_____
_____
_____

3. _____
_____
_____
_____

4. _____
_____
_____
_____

5. _____
_____
_____
_____

Today I am letting go of..

_____
_____
_____
_____

Date: __/__/__

Rephrase negative thoughts/habits I have into positive Thank You's
Let's reprogram our mind, by reprogramming our thoughts!

1._____
_____
_____
_____

2._____
_____
_____
_____

3._____
_____
_____
_____

4._____
_____
_____
_____

5._____
_____
_____
_____

"Every thought of yours is a real thing - a force" -Prentice Mulford

Thoughts become things! Before we can begin manifesting our reality, we must learn to reprogram our thoughts. After all, manifesting is thinking (thoughts become things). The reason people don't have what they want is because they are constantly focused on just that - what they **don't** have. If we reprogram our mind to be grateful for what we **do** have and turn those negative thoughts into positive ones, we will begin to think of what we **do** have and what we **do** want, rather than the opposite. That is when life begins to change - opportunity enters, abundance fills our lives and we become who we are meant to be.

Scripting

Before we begin, take a few moments to close your eyes and breathe. Imagine that you are exactly where you want to be. Whether that is in your new home, on your dream vacation, driving your dream car, etc. Picture yourself there, feel the gratitude, the excitement, the love for being exactly where you've always dreamed of being. Picture every detail vividly. Take as much time as you need and when you are ready, open your eyes and write about it! Write as if you're still there, list every possible detail, the more the better. Write in the present tense as if you're there right now. For example, if you want to manifest your dream apartment, as I did, write as if you have just moved in. "Wow! I cannot believe I am sitting here, on the balcony of my dream apartment in New York City. I've been dreaming of moving here for so long and here I am, on my own private balcony with the view of the Freedom Tower!! My new apartment is everything I've imagined and more. The kitchen is incredible, with a huge white marble island in the middle. I feel so grateful and excited..." Continue by writing down all of the details. What chair are you sitting on as you're writing? What does the apartment look like? List every detail. How many bedrooms are there? How did it feel unpacking and organizing all of your things? Did all of your furniture deliver or are you still shopping for it? etc.

Be sure to write in the present or past tense - as if it's already done - because it is already done. Writing in the future tense attracts the energy of "I want" or "it will happen" but this is already done.

Use the next few pages to write about what is already done for you!

This page was left blank intentionally to continue your list if needed

This page was left blank intentionally to continue your list if needed

This page was left blank intentionally to continue your list if needed

This page was left blank intentionally to continue your list if needed

This page was left blank intentionally to continue your list if needed

"Cultivate an optimistic mind, use your imagination, always consider alternatives, and dare to believe that you can make possible what others think is impossible."
-Rodolfo Costa

Week 4 will be dedicated to discovering and taking back our own power.

Use the next week to focus on your thoughts about yourself, how you speak about yourself and what you project about yourself.

Choose your thoughts and words about yourself carefully. Remember, you attract what you are in harmonious vibration with!

Becoming an Energetic Match

Are you an energetic match for your desires? Where can we clean up loose energy?

For the past few weeks, we've been working on becoming an energetic match for our desires! We've been getting clear on what it is we want, shifting our beliefs to understand that what we want is ours, focusing on gratitude so we have more to be grateful for and working on **be**-ing the person we want to be.

Last week, we worked on "Scripting". Everything you wrote down is already done, it's already yours because you brought it into reality through your thoughts. It exists in the Quantum and now you are just waiting for it to manifest physically on this 3D Earth. It is energy that is shifting into form. With this in mind, let go of any and all worry and rest in knowing that all that you want is already yours.
Truly knowing this is already yours allows you to just be. Be the person you would be if this was all yours, because it is! In being this person, you have what this person has. This is all we've been working on up until now - **be**-ing in order to attract - because you can only attract that which you are.

We've already worked on who this person is, what characteristics they posses. The question now is, are you being this person? Do you posses these characteristics? Are you doing the things you wrote down previously in "Understanding your current results" and "Getting into Alignment"?

Becoming an Energetic Match

In order to become an energetic match, we must be the energy. If you were a billionaire, would you really be worrying about the $100 you spent earlier today? Or the credit card bill that is higher than you anticipated? No, you would carry on and feel at peace knowing that you are a billionaire and you make more money than you know what to do with. So act this way now, as if it is already done, because it is!

Again, all that we want is already ours. It is done in the quantum! If you can understand and trust that, you have nothing to worry about! It is yours, in divine timing. So, rest in this knowledge and let all other thoughts that tell you otherwise, pass right through you.

All of the work we've done up until now has been physical, inspired action to help bring down our manifestations to this 3D realm called earth. We've been getting in tune with our higher selves, with truth. Now what?

We continue with inspired action, because this is how we continue to be an energetic match.

Here are a few questions to help activate inspired action:

What do I feel called to do right now?
What feels good right now?
What can I do today to help align my goals?

Ask yourself these questions everyday for the next week. Take time to do things that feel right in the moment.

Becoming an Energetic Match

The more you ask yourself these questions and follow through with what comes to you, the easier it will be to hear and trust your intuition (your higher self).

In the section entitled "Getting into Alignment" You were asked to state three goals and then an action step for each goal. Have you been taking these actions? Maybe new action steps are coming to you now. Write them down. What do you feel called to do right now? Your goals are your goals for a reason - you were guided to these goals by your higher self because they were meant to be achieved by you. You hold all of the answers to achieving these goals, you just need to lean in and trust yourself.
What do you feel called to do right now?

_____
_____
_____
_____
_____
_____
_____
_____
_____
_____
_____
_____
_____
_____

Becoming an Energetic Match

The most important part of becoming an energetic match, is staying an energetic match. How can we stay in the energy of a billionaire?

First, we must remember what we learned early on in this journal, our current results are based on our previous thoughts. Our future results are based on our current thoughts. Whenever a thought arrives that does not align with the energy you are looking to attract, ask yourself "Who do these thoughts belong to?" Ask yourself a few times, until you release these thoughts.

Next, create an energy shifting list (below). What can you do to shift the energy that does not align with your higher self. Come back to this list when you feel your energy is out of alignment.

10 Minutes or Less:
Examples: Take a few deep breaths, Take a 10 minute walk, 10 minute meditation, 10 min podcast, etc.

_____

_____

_____

_____

10 Minutes or More:
Examples: Call a loved one, 30-45 minute journal session, workout, bath, listen to a podcast, etc.

_____

_____

_____

_____

Week IV

My main goal for this week is...

_____

_____

_____

_____

_____

I am achieving my goal by...

_____

_____

_____

_____

Words of Affirmation

I Am _____

I Am _____

I Am _____

I Am _____

I Am _____

Date: __/__/__

Morning Prompt: *Thank you for waking me up to a new, incredible day*
(read this out loud or say it in your head)

I am truly grateful for _____ (because)

1. _____
   _____
   _____
   _____

2. _____
   _____
   _____
   _____

3. _____
   _____
   _____
   _____

4. _____
   _____
   _____
   _____

5. _____
   _____
   _____
   _____

Today I am letting go of..

_____
_____
_____
_____

Date: __/__/__

Rephrase negative thoughts/habits I have into positive Thank You's

Let's reprogram our mind, by reprogramming our thoughts!

1. _____
_____
_____
_____

2. _____
_____
_____
_____

3. _____
_____
_____
_____

4. _____
_____
_____
_____

5. _____
_____
_____
_____

"Every thought of yours is a real thing - a force" -Prentice Mulford

Thoughts become things! Before we can begin manifesting our reality, we must learn to reprogram our thoughts. After all, manifesting is thinking (thoughts become things). The reason people don't have what they want is because they are constantly focused on just that - what they **don't** have. If we reprogram our mind to be grateful for what we **do** have and turn those negative thoughts into positive ones, we will begin to think of what we **do** have and what we **do** want, rather than the opposite. That is when life begins to change - opportunity enters, abundance fills our lives and we become who we are meant to be.

Meditation & Visualization

Following each daily entry, you'll be prompted to take a few minutes to yourself to take it all in. If you can, close your eyes and breathe.

Start by focusing on the things you wrote down - truly believe in those words, focus on the fruition of every 'Thank you' you've written down. See it physically come to life, picture it in your mind. How do you feel? Feel the excitement, the happiness, feel every positive emotion you can as you vividly imagine your perfect life.

Finally, focus on the sound of your breath and how your body moves with every inhale and exhale for a few moments. Feel the calmness. Feel the revitalization.

As you continue this process on a daily basis, you are starting to plant seeds into your subconscious mind. The more you believe and feel what you are saying, the faster the seeds you plant will grow. When you can envision the outcome of what you're hoping for, as if it has already happened, your conscious mind will start to believe it and relay the information to your subconscious mind. Your subconscious mind turns these thoughts into a reality!

"The beginning of a habit is like an invisible thread, but every time we repeat the act we strengthen the strand, add to it another filament, until it becomes a great cable and binds us irrevocably, thought and act."
-Orison Swett Marden

Date: __/__/__

I am truly grateful for _____ (because)

1. _____
_____
_____
_____

2. _____
_____
_____
_____

3. _____
_____
_____
_____

4. _____
_____
_____
_____

5. _____
_____
_____
_____

Today I am letting go of..

_____
_____
_____
_____

Date: __/__/__

Rephrase negative thoughts/habits I have into positive Thank You's

Let's reprogram our mind, by reprogramming our thoughts!

1. _____
   _____
   _____
   _____

2. _____
   _____
   _____
   _____

3. _____
   _____
   _____
   _____

4. _____
   _____
   _____
   _____

5. _____
   _____
   _____
   _____

"Every thought of yours is a real thing - a force" -Prentice Mulford

Thoughts become things! Before we can begin manifesting our reality, we must learn to reprogram our thoughts. After all, manifesting is thinking (thoughts become things). The reason people don't have what they want is because they are constantly focused on just that - what they **don't** have. If we reprogram our mind to be grateful for what we **do** have and turn those negative thoughts into positive ones, we will begin to think of what we **do** have and what we **do** want, rather than the opposite. That is when life begins to change - opportunity enters, abundance fills our lives and we become who we are meant to be.

"We are what we think.
All that we are arises
with our thoughts.
With our thoughts, we
make our world"
-The Buddha

Date: __/__/__

I am truly grateful for _____ (because)

1. _____
_____
_____
_____

2. _____
_____
_____
_____

3. _____
_____
_____
_____

4. _____
_____
_____
_____

5. _____
_____
_____
_____

Today I am letting go of..

_____
_____
_____
_____

Rephrase negative thoughts/habits I have into positive Thank You's

Let's reprogram our mind, by reprogramming our thoughts!

1. _____

   _____

   _____

   _____

2. _____

   _____

   _____

   _____

3. _____

   _____

   _____

   _____

4. _____

   _____

   _____

   _____

5. _____

   _____

   _____

   _____

"Every thought of yours is a real thing - a force" -Prentice Mulford

Thoughts become things! Before we can begin manifesting our reality, we must learn to reprogram our thoughts. After all, manifesting is thinking (thoughts become things). The reason people don't have what they want is because they are constantly focused on just that - what they **don't** have. If we reprogram our mind to be grateful for what we **do** have and turn those negative thoughts into positive ones, we will begin to think of what we **do** have and what we **do** want, rather than the opposite. That is when life begins to change - opportunity enters, abundance fills our lives and we become who we are meant to be.

"It is the mind that maketh good of ill, that maketh wretch or happy, rich or poor."
-Edmund Spenser

Date: __/__/__

Morning Prompt: *Thank you for waking me up to a new, incredible day*
(read this out loud or say it in your head)

I am truly grateful for _____ (because)

1. _____
   _____
   _____
   _____

2. _____
   _____
   _____
   _____

3. _____
   _____
   _____
   _____

4. _____
   _____
   _____
   _____

5. _____
   _____
   _____
   _____

Today I am letting go of..

_____
_____
_____
_____

Date: __/__/__

Rephrase negative thoughts/habits I have into positive Thank You's

Let's reprogram our mind, by reprogramming our thoughts!

1._____
_____
_____
_____

2._____
_____
_____
_____

3._____
_____
_____
_____

4._____
_____
_____
_____

5._____
_____
_____
_____

"Every thought of yours is a real thing - a force" -Prentice Mulford

Thoughts become things! Before we can begin manifesting our reality, we must learn to reprogram our thoughts. After all, manifesting is thinking (thoughts become things). The reason people don't have what they want is because they are constantly focused on just that - what they **don't** have. If we reprogram our mind to be grateful for what we **do** have and turn those negative thoughts into positive ones, we will begin to think of what we **do** have and what we **do** want, rather than the opposite. That is when life begins to change - opportunity enters, abundance fills our lives and we become who we are meant to be.

"When you arise in the morning think of what a privilege it is to be alive, to think, to enjoy, to love."
-Marcus Aurelius

Morning Prompt: *Thank you for waking me up to a new, incredible day*
(read this out loud or say it in your head)

I am truly grateful for _____ (because)

1. _____
_____
_____
_____

2. _____
_____
_____
_____

3. _____
_____
_____
_____

4. _____
_____
_____
_____

5. _____
_____
_____
_____

Today I am letting go of..

_____
_____
_____
_____

Date: __/__/__

Rephrase negative thoughts/habits I have into positive Thank You's

Let's reprogram our mind, by reprogramming our thoughts!

1. _____
   _____
   _____
   _____

2. _____
   _____
   _____
   _____

3. _____
   _____
   _____
   _____

4. _____
   _____
   _____
   _____

5. _____
   _____
   _____
   _____

"Every thought of yours is a real thing - a force" -Prentice Mulford

Thoughts become things! Before we can begin manifesting our reality, we must learn to reprogram our thoughts. After all, manifesting is thinking (thoughts become things). The reason people don't have what they want is because they are constantly focused on just that - what they **don't** have. If we reprogram our mind to be grateful for what we **do** have and turn those negative thoughts into positive ones, we will begin to think of what we **do** have and what we **do** want, rather than the opposite. That is when life begins to change - opportunity enters, abundance fills our lives and we become who we are meant to be.

"It is only with gratitude that life becomes rich."
-Dietrich Bonhoeffer

Date: __/__/__

Morning Prompt: *Thank you for waking me up to a new, incredible day*
(read this out loud or say it in your head)

I am truly grateful for _____ (because)

1. _____
_____
_____
_____

2. _____
_____
_____
_____

3. _____
_____
_____
_____

4. _____
_____
_____
_____

5. _____
_____
_____
_____

Today I am letting go of..

_____
_____
_____
_____

Date: __/__/__

Rephrase negative thoughts/habits I have into positive Thank You's

Let's reprogram our mind, by reprogramming our thoughts!

1. _____
_____
_____
_____

2. _____
_____
_____
_____

3. _____
_____
_____
_____

4. _____
_____
_____
_____

5. _____
_____
_____
_____

"Every thought of yours is a real thing - a force" -Prentice Mulford

Thoughts become things! Before we can begin manifesting our reality, we must learn to reprogram our thoughts. After all, manifesting is thinking (thoughts become things). The reason people don't have what they want is because they are constantly focused on just that - what they **don't** have. If we reprogram our mind to be grateful for what we **do** have and turn those negative thoughts into positive ones, we will begin to think of what we **do** have and what we **do** want, rather than the opposite. That is when life begins to change - opportunity enters, abundance fills our lives and we become who we are meant to be.

"We become what we think about most of the time, and that's the strangest secret."
-Earl Nightingale

Date: __/__/__

Morning Prompt: *Thank you for waking me up to a new, incredible day*
(read this out loud or say it in your head)

I am truly grateful for _____ (because)

1. _____

_____

_____

_____

2. _____

_____

_____

_____

3. _____

_____

_____

_____

4. _____

_____

_____

_____

5. _____

_____

_____

_____

Today I am letting go of..

_____

_____

_____

_____

Date: __/__/__

Rephrase negative thoughts/habits I have into positive Thank You's

Let's reprogram our mind, by reprogramming our thoughts!

1. _____
_____
_____
_____

2. _____
_____
_____
_____

3. _____
_____
_____
_____

4. _____
_____
_____
_____

5. _____
_____
_____
_____

"Every thought of yours is a real thing - a force" -Prentice Mulford

Thoughts become things! Before we can begin manifesting our reality, we must learn to reprogram our thoughts. After all, manifesting is thinking (thoughts become things). The reason people don't have what they want is because they are constantly focused on just that - what they **don't** have. If we reprogram our mind to be grateful for what we **do** have and turn those negative thoughts into positive ones, we will begin to think of what we **do** have and what we **do** want, rather than the opposite. That is when life begins to change - opportunity enters, abundance fills our lives and we become who we are meant to be.

The Power of I Am

We are constantly stating who we are and who we are not. Everything we say binds us. You get to choose who you are because you get to choose what you say. When you say "I am ....." you are declaring that which you are (and that which you attract).

For example, if you are constantly saying "I am tired" or "I am exhausted" you will continue to attract things that make you tired or exhausted.

Pay attention to what you say after "I am.." because that is what you are attracting. In the same way, when you say "I want" you are also saying "I don't have" because you are in a state of want. By saying "I want" you are saying "I am not" and therefore you are attracting more of what you are not.

It's time to shift these thoughts and statements to remove yourself from the false identities you are creating about yourself. Rather than saying "I am tired" say "I perceive the feeling of tiredness". This statement will help you understand that it is not you who is tired, it is you who perceives the feeling of being tired. It will also remind you to choose your words carefully.

Use the next page to state that which you are - and that which you attract. Here are some examples I use on a daily basis:
I am abundance personified
I am healthy, wealthy and happy
I am perfectly healthy, all of the cells, tissues and organs in my body work in perfect harmony
I am divine and I have everything that I desire

The Power of I Am

Now it's your turn. Remember, everything we say binds us. Who are you?

_____
_____
_____
_____
_____
_____
_____
_____
_____
_____
_____
_____
_____
_____
_____
_____
_____
_____
_____
_____
_____
_____
_____
_____
_____
_____

"The attitude a person develops is the most important ingredient in determining the level of success... People who are negatively conditioned accept defeat. People who are positive don't."
-Pat Riley

We are approaching the final week. Week 5 will be dedicated to helping you understand your power.

Use the next week to focus on how far you've come! Be grateful for all of the lessons along the way and all of the lessons to come.

Take time for yourself every night this week to attract what you desire, by **be**-ing the energy you want to attract. Remember, you attract what you are in harmonious vibration with!

Feeling Is The Secret

Over the past few weeks, we've begun the journey of changing our perception to a more positive one, in order to change our vibration (feeling) and therefore our frequency to match the frequency of our desires. Through gratitude, we've been able to raise our vibration, and attract more to be grateful for.

We've dug deep and exposed many of our limiting beliefs, then we rewrote these beliefs in the same way we wanted to rewrite these areas of our lives. Up until now, we have learned that we are made up of energy and that like everything else, our thoughts are also made up of energy.

** If you haven't been doing so on a weekly basis, take a few minutes to reread the first 9 pages of this journal.

Our thoughts **and** feelings determine the frequency we vibrate at. We've rewritten our beliefs in order to change our perception, but now we must combine these thoughts with feeling.

How can we really feel all that we've been writing and saying? The answer lies within us - through our imagination. Go back and read everything you wrote down in the "Scripting" section. Close your eyes and feel what you just read - actually feel it all in your mind. I want you to get to the point where you're lost in your imagination, so much so, that you forget where you physically are in this moment. When you get to this stage, think about yourself now in this moment, as if it were in the past. Remember you in this moment dreaming about where you are (in your imagination). See the example on the next page.

Feeling Is The Secret

Example: I'm currently sitting on the couch in my current living room. I just reread everything I wrote in the "Scripting" section and now I am closing my eyes imaging myself in my new NYC apartment, sitting on the balcony after just moving in all of my stuff. I picture myself getting up from the chair in the balcony and putting my journal down, going inside the apartment and starting to unbox all of my kitchenware. I am picturing myself feeling the plates as I take them out of the box and place them on my new beautiful white marble kitchen island. As I move the plates from the island to the cabinet I remember the moment I was sitting on my couch in my previous living room, dreaming about this very moment. I am filled with love and gratitude. I am in awe of the fact that I created this reality and am now living in the moment I once dreamt of. I start to play music and dance in my new home, I smile and laugh as I feel all of the feelings of joy, excitement, gratitude and support from the universe.

Continue for as long as you want, until you're completely lost in this space, feeling every feeling. The more vividly you feel, the more energy you call in.

Do this exercise every day at least once. If possible, do it twice. The best time to do this would be right before bed, when your body is deeply relaxed, your conscious mind is at rest and your subconscious mind is most accessible. I recommend doing this about 30 minutes earlier than you would normally go to bed, so that you don't fall asleep.

Week V

My main goal for this week is...

_____

_____

_____

_____

I am achieving my goal by...

_____

_____

_____

_____

Words of Affirmation

I Am _____

I Am _____

I Am _____

I Am _____

I Am _____

Date: __/__/__

I am truly grateful for _____ (because)

1. _____
   _____
   _____
   _____

2. _____
   _____
   _____
   _____

3. _____
   _____
   _____
   _____

4. _____
   _____
   _____
   _____

5. _____
   _____
   _____
   _____

Today I am letting go of..

_____
_____
_____
_____

Date: __/__/__

Rephrase negative thoughts/habits I have into positive Thank You's

Let's reprogram our mind, by reprogramming our thoughts!

1. _____
_____
_____
_____

2. _____
_____
_____
_____

3. _____
_____
_____
_____

4. _____
_____
_____
_____

5. _____
_____
_____
_____

"Every thought of yours is a real thing - a force" -Prentice Mulford

Thoughts become things! Before we can begin manifesting our reality, we must learn to reprogram our thoughts. After all, manifesting is thinking (thoughts become things). The reason people don't have what they want is because they are constantly focused on just that - what they **don't** have. If we reprogram our mind to be grateful for what we **do** have and turn those negative thoughts into positive ones, we will begin to think of what we **do** have and what we **do** want, rather than the opposite. That is when life begins to change - opportunity enters, abundance fills our lives and we become who we are meant to be.

Meditation & Visualization

Following each daily entry, you'll be prompted to take a few minutes to yourself to take it all in. If you can, close your eyes and breathe.

Start by focusing on the things you wrote down - truly believe in those words, focus on the fruition of every 'Thank you' you've written down. See it physically come to life, picture it in your mind. How do you feel? Feel the excitement, the happiness, feel every positive emotion you can as you vividly imagine your perfect life.

Finally, focus on the sound of your breath and how your body moves with every inhale and exhale for a few moments. Feel the calmness. Feel the revitalization.

As you continue this process on a daily basis, you are starting to plant seeds into your subconscious mind. The more you believe and feel what you are saying, the faster the seeds you plant will grow. When you can envision the outcome of what you're hoping for, as if it has already happened, your conscious mind will start to believe it and relay the information to your subconscious mind. Your subconscious mind turns these thoughts into a reality!

"If my mind can conceive it, if my heart can believe it, then I can achieve it."
-Muhammad Ali

Date: __/__/__

I am truly grateful for _____ (because)

1. _____
_____
_____
_____

2. _____
_____
_____
_____

3. _____
_____
_____
_____

4. _____
_____
_____
_____

5. _____
_____
_____
_____

Today I am letting go of..

_____
_____
_____
_____

Date: __/__/__

Rephrase negative thoughts/habits I have into positive Thank You's

Let's reprogram our mind, by reprogramming our thoughts!

1. _____
   _____
   _____
   _____

2. _____
   _____
   _____
   _____

3. _____
   _____
   _____
   _____

4. _____
   _____
   _____
   _____

5. _____
   _____
   _____
   _____

"Every thought of yours is a real thing - a force" -Prentice Mulford

Thoughts become things! Before we can begin manifesting our reality, we must learn to reprogram our thoughts. After all, manifesting is thinking (thoughts become things). The reason people don't have what they want is because they are constantly focused on just that - what they **don't** have. If we reprogram our mind to be grateful for what we **do** have and turn those negative thoughts into positive ones, we will begin to think of what we **do** have and what we **do** want, rather than the opposite. That is when life begins to change - opportunity enters, abundance fills our lives and we become who we are meant to be.

"Things have a way of working themselves out if we just remain positive."
-Lou Holtz

Date: __/__/__

Morning Prompt: *Thank you for waking me up to a new, incredible day*
(read this out loud or say it in your head)

I am truly grateful for _____ (because)

1. _____
_____
_____
_____

2. _____
_____
_____
_____

3. _____
_____
_____
_____

4. _____
_____
_____
_____

5. _____
_____
_____
_____

Today I am letting go of..

_____
_____
_____
_____

Date: __/__/__

Rephrase negative thoughts/habits I have into positive Thank You's

Let's reprogram our mind, by reprogramming our thoughts!

1. _____
_____
_____
_____

2. _____
_____
_____
_____

3. _____
_____
_____
_____

4. _____
_____
_____
_____

5. _____
_____
_____
_____

"Every thought of yours is a real thing - a force" -Prentice Mulford

Thoughts become things! Before we can begin manifesting our reality, we must learn to reprogram our thoughts. After all, manifesting is thinking (thoughts become things). The reason people don't have what they want is because they are constantly focused on just that - what they **don't** have. If we reprogram our mind to be grateful for what we **do** have and turn those negative thoughts into positive ones, we will begin to think of what we **do** have and what we **do** want, rather than the opposite. That is when life begins to change - opportunity enters, abundance fills our lives and we become who we are meant to be.

"I don't think anything is unrealistic if you believe you can do it."
-Mike Ditka

Date: __/__/__

I am truly grateful for _____ (because)

1. _____
_____
_____
_____

2. _____
_____
_____
_____

3. _____
_____
_____
_____

4. _____
_____
_____
_____

5. _____
_____
_____
_____

Today I am letting go of..

_____
_____
_____
_____

Date: __/__/__

Rephrase negative thoughts/habits I have into positive Thank You's

Let's reprogram our mind, by reprogramming our thoughts!

1. _____
_____
_____
_____

2. _____
_____
_____
_____

3. _____
_____
_____
_____

4. _____
_____
_____
_____

5. _____
_____
_____
_____

"Every thought of yours is a real thing - a force" -Prentice Mulford

Thoughts become things! Before we can begin manifesting our reality, we must learn to reprogram our thoughts. After all, manifesting is thinking (thoughts become things). The reason people don't have what they want is because they are constantly focused on just that - what they **don't** have. If we reprogram our mind to be grateful for what we **do** have and turn those negative thoughts into positive ones, we will begin to think of what we **do** have and what we **do** want, rather than the opposite. That is when life begins to change - opportunity enters, abundance fills our lives and we become who we are meant to be.

"Success is the sum of small efforts, repeated day-in and day-out."
-Robert Collier

Date: __/__/__

I am truly grateful for _____ (because)

1. _____
_____
_____
_____

2. _____
_____
_____
_____

3. _____
_____
_____
_____

4. _____
_____
_____
_____

5. _____
_____
_____
_____

Today I am letting go of..

_____
_____
_____
_____

Date: __/__/__

Rephrase negative thoughts/habits I have into positive Thank You's

Let's reprogram our mind, by reprogramming our thoughts!

1. _____
_____
_____
_____

2. _____
_____
_____
_____

3. _____
_____
_____
_____

4. _____
_____
_____
_____

5. _____
_____
_____
_____

"Every thought of yours is a real thing - a force" -Prentice Mulford

Thoughts become things! Before we can begin manifesting our reality, we must learn to reprogram our thoughts. After all, manifesting is thinking (thoughts become things). The reason people don't have what they want is because they are constantly focused on just that - what they **don't** have. If we reprogram our mind to be grateful for what we **do** have and turn those negative thoughts into positive ones, we will begin to think of what we **do** have and what we **do** want, rather than the opposite. That is when life begins to change - opportunity enters, abundance fills our lives and we become who we are meant to be.

"Being what most people think is realistic is only a way of justifying negative thinking. Go for something great."
-Dr. Bob Rotella

Date: __/__/__

I am truly grateful for _____ (because)

1. _____
_____
_____
_____

2. _____
_____
_____
_____

3. _____
_____
_____
_____

4. _____
_____
_____
_____

5. _____
_____
_____
_____

Today I am letting go of..

_____
_____
_____
_____

Date: __/__/__

Rephrase negative thoughts/habits I have into positive Thank You's

Let's reprogram our mind, by reprogramming our thoughts!

1. _____
   _____
   _____
   _____

2. _____
   _____
   _____
   _____

3. _____
   _____
   _____
   _____

4. _____
   _____
   _____
   _____

5. _____
   _____
   _____
   _____

"Every thought of yours is a real thing - a force" -Prentice Mulford

Thoughts become things! Before we can begin manifesting our reality, we must learn to reprogram our thoughts. After all, manifesting is thinking (thoughts become things). The reason people don't have what they want is because they are constantly focused on just that - what they **don't** have. If we reprogram our mind to be grateful for what we **do** have and turn those negative thoughts into positive ones, we will begin to think of what we **do** have and what we **do** want, rather than the opposite. That is when life begins to change - opportunity enters, abundance fills our lives and we become who we are meant to be.

"Live life to the fullest and focus on the positive."
-Matt Cameron

Date: __/__/__

I am truly grateful for _____ (because)

1. _____
   _____
   _____
   _____

2. _____
   _____
   _____
   _____

3. _____
   _____
   _____
   _____

4. _____
   _____
   _____
   _____

5. _____
   _____
   _____
   _____

Today I am letting go of..

_____
_____
_____
_____

Date: __/__/__

Rephrase negative thoughts/habits I have into positive Thank You's

Let's reprogram our mind, by reprogramming our thoughts!

1. _____
_____
_____
_____

2. _____
_____
_____
_____

3. _____
_____
_____
_____

4. _____
_____
_____
_____

5. _____
_____
_____
_____

"*Every thought of yours is a real thing - a force*" -Prentice Mulford

Thoughts become things! Before we can begin manifesting our reality, we must learn to reprogram our thoughts. After all, manifesting is thinking (thoughts become things). The reason people don't have what they want is because they are constantly focused on just that - what they **don't** have. If we reprogram our mind to be grateful for what we **do** have and turn those negative thoughts into positive ones, we will begin to think of what we **do** have and what we **do** want, rather than the opposite. That is when life begins to change - opportunity enters, abundance fills our lives and we become who we are meant to be.

The How Isn't For You

How many things have you manifested up util now? Good or bad? The truth is your entire life is manifestation after manifestation, based on your thoughts and feelings.

For all of the good things that you've manifested, did you know exactly when and how it was going to work out? or did it just work out?

Worrying about how and when will only attract more worry. Remember, you attract what you are. If you are worrying, you attract more to worry about. If you are relaxed and happy knowing that what you want is already yours, that is what you will attract. Just like you cannot be in two places at once, your consciousness cannot be in two places. You are either sure it's going to happen, or you're worrying about if, when and how it will happen. You get to choose where you place your consciousness. It's one or the other, you attract what you are. Are you worried? or Are you sure (that what you want is already yours)?

Neville Goddard talks about The Law of Assumption, or the feeling of the wish fulfilled. Persist in your assumption, feel your desire as if it has already been fulfilled and be the person you would be if it was so.

If your response to this is "I've been assuming this for such and such time and I still don't have it" then that is your assumption - you're assuming you don't have it.

The Law of Assumption

Either you do have it - because you assume it and you're waiting for the perfect timing and perfect circumstances in which it arrives - or you assume that you don't have it, because it is not physically here right now. Therefore, if you assume you don't have it - because it is not physically here right now - then your assumption is that it is not yours, so you don't have it in the future either.

Most people fail to apply The Law of Assumption successfully because they do not maintain the feeling long enough for it to appear before them. They do not persist in it, and instead they allow their senses and the physical world to convince them that it is not realistic or possible for them. Remember, our current results are based on our past thoughts. Our future results are based on our current thoughts - you get to choose! The choice is always yours, you are the creator of your own destiny!

Just as you have been up until now, throughout this journal, you must choose and revise your thoughts carefully. You must be in the conscious of having something in order to have it. Let go of any and all worry. Let go of any and all "what ifs". Only when you can maintain the feeling, despite all physical evidence to the contrary, will you be able to manifest that which you have chosen for yourself.

The choice is yours. It has always been yours.

Choose Your Thoughts

This entire journal was created to help you realize the power that resides inside of you. It's the same power that resides in all of us.

We can choose to worry or we can choose to just observe these thoughts of worry and let them pass right through us. We can choose to know that what we desire is already ours. It's done.

Choose your thoughts and choose what thoughts you give energy to. You attract what you are. You attract what you give energy to.

Remember, "I am..".

You get to choose who you are.
You've chosen up until now.
Who will you choose to be from now on?

"Cultivate an optimistic mind, use your imagination, always consider alternatives, and dare to believe that you can make possible what others think is impossible."
-Rodolfo Costa

Front cover image by Robert Ulaj
Book design by Robert Ulaj

First Printing Edition 2022.